Racing Sled Dogs

By riding low on his sled, this driver is helping his team go faster, shaving seconds off of his finishing time.

Racing Sled Dogs

An Original North American Sport

by Michael Cooper

Illustrated with photographs and drawings

Clarion Books

TICKNOR & FIELDS: A HOUGHTON MIFFLIN COMPANY

New York

Photo credits appear on page 67.

The author gratefully acknowledges some of the people who made this book possible: Russell Freedman; Bart Campbell and Dan Church, ALPO Petfoods; Harris and Ginger Dunlap; Roberta A. Vesley, American Kennel Club; Donna Hawley, International Sled Dog Racing Association; and Richard H. Engeman, University of Washington Libraries.

Map by Susan Detrich

Clarion Books
Ticknor & Fields, a Houghton Mifflin Company
Text copyright © 1988 by Michael Cooper
All rights reserved.
For information about permission to reproduce
selections from this book, write to Permissions,
Houghton Mifflin Company, 2 Park Street, Boston, MA 02108
Printed in the U.S.A.

Library of Congress Cataloging-in-Publication Data
Cooper, Michael, 1950–
    Racing sled dogs.

    Includes index.
    Summary: Text and photographs describe the sport
of sled dog racing, focusing on the Iditarod race in
Alaska and discussing how dogs are raised and trained
as racers, the history of sled dog racing, and how the
sport is practiced in North America.
    1. Sled dog racing — Juvenile literature.
2. Sled dogs — Juvenile literature. 3. Iditarod Trail
Sled Dog Race, Alaska — Juvenile literature. [1. Sled
dog racing. 2. Sled dogs. 3. Iditarod Trail Sled Dog
Race, Alaska] I. Title.
SF440.15.C66 1988   798'.8   87-25007
ISBN 0-89919-499-0

P 10 9 8 7 6 5 4 3 2 1

For Richard

Contents

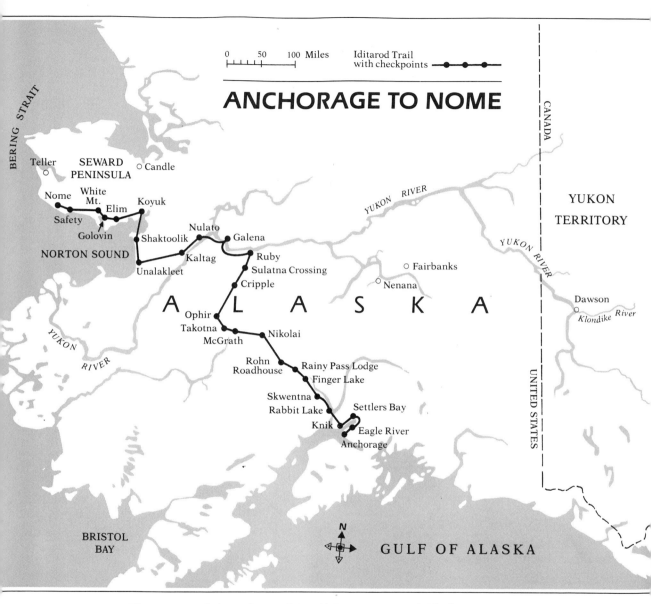

The route of the Iditarod Trail International Sled Dog Race.

1. Winning the Iditarod

Gusts of wind sixty miles an hour rocked the lone sled sitting on the frozen ocean. The air was white with snow, and the temperature was a bone-chilling thirty below zero. A sleeping bag stretched out on the back of the sled stirred, and out peeked Libby Riddles's blond head. She peered through the swirling snow at the still-raging storm and at her dogs curled up snugly by the sled.

This was the seventeenth day in the Iditarod (pronounced i-DIT-a-rod) Trail International Sled Dog Race, a race of some 1,100 miles across Alaska's winter wilderness from Anchorage to Nome. Now, in her third Iditarod, twenty-nine-year-old Libby Riddles was close to realizing her biggest dream — to win the race. Only two hundred miles from the finish line and in the lead, Libby felt sure of victory.

The 1985 Iditarod, like every Iditarod race, was a long test of endurance against nature's harshest weather and roughest terrain. Mushers, a term that Alaskans use for sled dog team drivers, had to plough through deep snow, endure below-zero temperatures, and avoid dangerous animals while guiding their sleds over mountains, through forests, and across frozen rivers.

The race began that year, as it does every year, on the first Saturday in March. Several days before the start, mushers began arriving in Anchorage, Alaska's largest city. All racers, both dogs and people, were examined by doctors. Mushers drew their starting positions from a boot.

Race rules required each sled to carry specific equipment: sleeping bag, axe, parka, food, snowshoes, and booties to protect the dogs' paws on hard, icy trails. Libby also took along her Sony Walkman with her favorite tapes.

She hitched up fifteen dogs, all three to three-and-a-half years old. They were Alaskan huskies. These dogs are usually a mix of Alaskan malamute, Siberian husky, and other breeds. Libby's dogs were taller and longer than some huskies because their ancestors included hounds, which are good running dogs. Many racing sled dogs are part hound.

Leading Libby's team were two brothers, Axel and Dugan. Lead dogs are the quarterbacks of a dog team. They're often exceptionally good sled dogs that guide and encourage the rest of the team.

On the morning of the race, the teams gathered in downtown Anchorage. It was quite a sight. Beside the modern buildings, hundreds of people — mushers, their helpers, and race officials — were busy packing sleds and checking equipment. About one thousand dogs, eager for the race to begin, jumped and yelped with excitement.

The race began promptly at nine that morning. Every

Libby is one of four women out of a total of sixty mushers to start in the 1985 Iditarod. A friend rides with her to the first checkpoint.

two minutes for over two hours, a team left Anchorage. The mushers followed a trail broken by snowmobiles and marked by stakes. The trail headed north toward the towering peaks of the Alaska Range. The length of the trail and the time it takes all of the racers to complete the race vary somewhat each year because of the weather. That year the finish line in Nome was about three weeks and 1,100 miles away — nearly the same distance as from Houston to Chicago.

After training all year, Libby felt thrilled at finally being on the Iditarod Trail. But bad luck soon dashed her high spirits. First, she took a wrong turn. Libby immediately realized her mistake, but it was hard turning around fifteen excited dogs. Then she discovered that her sled's brake was broken and needed to be replaced. But these were minor problems compared with what happened next — near disaster.

After the first seven hours on the trail, Libby stopped to rest and to give her dogs a snack. She tied the team to a small tree. The dogs were still very excited, and they jumped and pulled as other teams raced by. They wanted to run, too. The strong dogs pulled down the tree, and before Libby could untie the rope, they surged ahead, dragging sled, tree, and Libby face first through the snow.

What do you do when you're being pulled through the snow by a team of dogs that you love and value more than anything else? Hang on and shout, Whoa! Whoa! That's exactly what Libby did, but her dogs were so excited and eager to run that they paid no attention.

Even pulling a driver and loaded sled, a team of fifteen dogs can sprint up to twenty miles an hour. Bravely, Libby hung on to the rope as long as she could. Exhausted, she eventually had to let go and watch her team disappear down the trail. Weighed down by a heavy coat and boots, she trudged through the deep snow hoping to catch up with her team. She worried that one of her dogs would become tangled in the harness and break a leg or, worse yet, strangle.

A musher stopped and gave Libby a ride. Such generosity was not surprising because mushers follow an unwritten code to help each other. They soon found her team. Another thoughtful musher, Terry Adkins, had tied the dogs to a tree, a deed that won him the Iditarod's annual good sportsmanship award.

After that nightmare of a beginning and nearly thirteen hours on the trail, Libby and her team arrived at the fourth checkpoint, Rabbit Lake, at one o'clock in the morning. Nothing more than a tent and several race officials, this was one of twenty-five checkpoints on the trail. The checkpoints served different purposes. At some, mushers were able to restock their supplies of food. At others, the teams were required to rest for a specific number of hours. And some checkpoints simply gave race officials a chance to see that the teams were safe and healthy.

Feeding dogs is a time-consuming part of the race. For three hours at Rabbit Lake, Libby cooked her team a big meal on a charcoal grill. Her race strategy was to fix hot food about every sixty miles. Race rules require each racer to carry on the sled two pounds of dog food for each dog and one day's food for the musher. Libby carried water and snacks of frozen meat and fish for her dogs. These foods are high in protein and carbohydrates, which give the dogs big doses of energy and help them work in the cold weather.

Like their dogs, mushers also need a high-energy diet. Libby snacked on dried moose meat. She also ate an Alaskan specialty called Eskimo ice cream, which is grated reindeer fat mixed with seal oil, salmonberries, and sugar.

Libby reached the Finger Lake checkpoint at two o'clock the next morning. She was stiff and sore from steering the heavy sled for twenty-four hours. Libby cooked food for her team and, while waiting for the sun to come up, grabbed a couple of hours' sleep in the back of her sled. She usually liked to travel at night, when it was very cold, so her dogs would not get too hot. But now she wanted to travel during the day, when she could see well, because the next part of the trail zigzagged down a steep and dangerous hill.

Going down steep hills can be treacherous. The dogs and the heavy sled go faster and faster. A sled's brake, which is a simple metal claw that digs into the snow, doesn't work well enough to stop the fast-moving sled. Libby kept her sled from going too fast by turning it on its side. Off its runners the sled doesn't slide as fast.

Eight hours after she left Finger Lake, Libby arrived at the next checkpoint, Rainy Pass Lodge. She was now 223 miles from Anchorage, where the race had started.

Iditarod racers get little sleep. This racer is taking a nap before hitting the trail again.

At Rainy Pass Lodge, Libby learned the race had been stopped by the officials because a snowstorm had grounded supply planes. The mushers had to stay at the checkpoint. They had little to do except complain, wait for better weather, and take care of their dogs. Libby rubbed her dogs' feet with ointment, which made them feel better after so many hours of pounding the trail. She worried about running out of food for her dogs. But another musher gave her a fifty-pound block of horse meat, which fed her team until supplies could be flown in.

The mushers stayed at Rainy Pass Lodge for three days while a storm dumped two more feet of snow on the ground. Then the weather cleared, and they hit the trail again. Going through the broad Ptarmigan Pass, Libby estimated the snow was six to eight feet deep, which forced the dogs to work extra hard. One musher, exaggerating only a little, said his team had to swim through the snow. The deep snow caused another musher to drop out of the race. He loved his dogs too much, he said, to make them work so hard.

Two days after leaving Rainy Pass Lodge, the teams raced for thirty miles along the frozen South Fork River. Here and on other sections of the trail that crossed frozen rivers, the mushers faced the constant danger of hitting thin ice and falling into the cold water. Getting wet in cold weather can cause hypothermia, a condition in which the body's temperature falls below normal. Hypothermia can kill a dog or a person.

Libby and the other mushers drove through exceptionally heavy snow and temperatures in the midthirties, which was too warm for thick-coated dogs to work in. Throughout the race, Libby was constantly concerned about the health of her team. Only a healthy team, she knew, could win. When several of her dogs had upset stomachs, she fed them rice. On the ninth day, when the race was stopped at Ophir (pronounced O-fer) for nearly twenty-four hours because of another snowstorm, Libby fed her dogs hot broth every few hours. Her tender, loving care paid off. When the race started up again, Libby's dogs were running well and enjoying themselves.

It's not unusual for dogs to become hurt or sick during the race. A dog that's unable to race is carried in the back of the sled until the team reaches a checkpoint where the dog can be left with race officials. Libby had to leave two of her dogs at checkpoints.

After fourteen days and seven hundred miles, Libby and the other racers were farther north. The temperature was forty below zero as the first of the mushers raced down the frozen, mile-wide Yukon River. Libby stayed in or near the lead. With two-thirds of the race behind her, Libby was beginning to feel the pressure of competition. She, and the other racers, too, worried most about Rick Swenson, a four-time winner of the Iditarod who had always run an excellent team.

Just before the Eskimo village of Shaktoolik (pronounced Shak-TOO-lik), about 225 miles from the finish line at Nome, a blinding Arctic storm blew up. Libby was used to this weather because her hometown of Teller, another Eskimo village, is north of Nome. During training she often drove her team fifty to sixty miles a day in the stiff winds on the frozen Bering Strait.

At the Shaktoolik checkpoint, Libby rested for three hours. As more mushers pulled into the village, Libby decided to take a dangerous chance. She and her team drove alone into the furious storm and approaching night to cross the frozen Norton Sound.

Out on the ice, the wind was gusting from forty to

sixty miles an hour. The strong wind blew snow across the ice and thirty feet into the air, creating what is known as a ground blizzard. Libby drove directly into the wind. Visibility was so bad she could barely see Axel and Dugan at the head of the team. She had to walk beside her sled to hunt for the trail markers. It was a tortuously slow journey. As night approached, Libby realized she was in danger of hitting thin ice or open water. That would mean almost certain death for her and the dogs.

After three hours, the team had traveled only fifteen miles. At one stop, the dogs decided that, at least for the time being, they had had enough. They curled up in the

Because she had dared to start across Norton Sound during a blizzard, Libby had a comfortable lead as she drew near to Nome.

snow, the tips of their tails warmly covering their noses. Her dogs, Libby figured, knew best. She climbed into her sleeping bag, wriggled out of her wet clothes, and tried to sleep as the fierce wind rocked her sled.

At seven thirty the next morning, Libby was up and prepared to continue the crossing. The wind, white with snow, blew fiercely. She fed her dogs a snack, and they were raring to go. For her own breakfast, Libby ate seal oil, Eskimo ice cream, and Norwegian chocolate.

The storm continued to rage. It took nearly nine hours to cross the sound, a trip that in good weather would take only a couple of hours. Libby finally reached the next checkpoint, the Eskimo village of Koyuk. After

that, it should have been a smooth trip through the last four checkpoints. But, because the trail markers were hidden by blowing snow, Libby went the wrong way.

She ended up in a village some ten miles off the trail. In other years, this kind of mistake had cost mushers the race. An Eskimo man showed Libby the trail to the right checkpoint, the village of Safety. He also told her not to worry because he had heard on the radio that the other mushers didn't have a chance of catching up with her.

After Safety, it was an easy twenty-two miles, about three hours, to Nome. The winner's welcome began while she was on the trail — Libby was greeted by snowmobiles carrying photographers. A helicopter hovered overhead, with a CBS television crew on board to film the finish.

At nine that morning in Nome, the fire siren let out a long wail to let everybody know that the first musher was about to finish the Iditarod. Nome's entire population, about three thousand people, rushed out of houses and restaurants. They lined both sides of Front Street, the town's main street, and cheered wildly as Libby and her team of thirteen dogs crossed the finish line. Libby Riddles had won the Iditarod after racing 1,172 miles in eighteen days and twenty minutes.

After ten years of building and training a team, Libby's dream to win the great race had become a reality. For winning the Iditarod, Libby received a check for fifty thousand dollars and a big silver bowl. But her best prize was a glass urn, the humanitarian award

Libby shares the winner's circle with her two lead dogs, Axel and Dugan.

given to the musher who takes the best care of his or her dogs during the race.

As the first woman to win the Iditarod, Libby had made history. Sixty years earlier, on the same street, another historic and heroic race over the Iditarod Trail had ended. It was the daring spirit of that earlier race that Libby and the other mushers of the Iditarod were honoring.

Gunnar Kasson and his team, shown in this 1925 photograph, completed the last fifty miles of the famous serum relay to Nome.

2. An Original North American Sport

Years before becoming famous for sled dog racing, the Iditarod Trail was an important supply route for northwestern Alaska. During long winter months, sled dog teams traveled the trail, delivering mail and supplies to remote towns and villages. The Iditarod Trail first became prominent in Alaska's history in 1925, when a dramatic relay by sled dog teams saved Nome from a deadly epidemic.

In that year, a diphtheria epidemic was spreading through Nome, threatening the town's ten thousand residents. The serum that could halt the epidemic was far away in Anchorage. It was January, a cold and dark month in the far north when ships can't sail because the ocean is frozen. At that time, airplanes were still crude machines unable to fly safely in Alaska's winter. The only way to deliver the serum to Nome was by dog team. A call for volunteers went out on short-wave radio, and over a dozen mushers living along the trail volunteered to relay the serum from a train stop at Nenana to Nome, 650 miles away.

U.S. Postal Service dog teams took three weeks to travel from one end of the Iditarod Trail to the other, but the serum relay teams couldn't afford that much time. Every day, people in Nome were dying from diphtheria. The mushers agreed to travel day and night. Leonhard Seppala, a well-known sled dog racing champion, made an exhausting five-hundred-mile nonstop round trip at the beginning of the relay to pick up the serum. The other mushers, to avoid getting too tired, each drove about fifty miles and then passed the serum on to a waiting team.

Despite short days and very cold weather, the relay went smoothly. On the next to last leg of the trip, just as Libby Riddles did sixty years later, a musher crossed frozen Norton Sound during a fierce storm. At five in the morning, only five-and-a-half days after the relay began, the serum arrived in Nome. Newspapers all across North America carried accounts of the dramatic relay.

A few years later, airplanes were built to withstand winter flying, and in Alaska they took over the job of delivering mail and supplies. As a result, the Iditarod Trail was almost forgotten until the late 1960s, when a group of Alaskans organized a long-distance sled dog race over the trail. The event would honor the spirit of the earlier mushers who had made the daring, lifesaving dash to Nome.

Since the first race in 1967, the Iditarod Trail International Sled Dog Race has become an annual event attracting worldwide attention.

Sled dog racing is an original North American sport. At the time of the serum relay it had been popular in Alaska for at least twenty years. Races were held in Canada as early as 1857, but they didn't influence the future of sled dog racing as much as early races in Nome.

At the turn of the century, Alaska was a U.S. district. The region was purchased from Russia in 1867, made a territory in 1912, and granted statehood in 1959. Nome was a bustling mining town that had sprung up in 1898 after gold was discovered nearby and twenty thousand people rushed to the Seward Peninsula hoping to find their fortunes.

Nome was full of dogs as well as prospectors. Dog teams worked gold mines, hauled supplies, and delivered the mail. With so many dog teams around, it was an obvious idea to have a little fun by holding a big race.

The Nome Kennel Club was organized to sponsor the first All Alaska Sweepstakes Race. First prize was ten thousand dollars. That's a lot of money today, but it was a lot more back in 1908 when most people didn't earn that much in several years of steady work. Following the telegraph wires from Nome to the town of Candle and back, ten teams raced 408 miles. The winner finished in five days.

Then, as today, the dogs were treated as prized athletes. The mushers carried little for themselves on their hickory and walrus-hide sleds except warm furs and boots. But for the dozen or more dogs in the team, there

A working team in Dawson City, Yukon Territory, in 1898, the height of the gold rush years.

were flannel moccasins to protect paws on hard, icy trails, dark veils to shade eyes from the strong sun, and blankets to shield bodies from the cutting wind.

Esther Birdsall Darling, president of the Nome Kennel Club in 1916, described how drivers treated their dogs: "In every resting place the dogs are considered first, and no man thinks of himself till his dogs are rubbed with alcohol, fed and bedded. . . . Many of the drivers sleep on the floor of the road-house with their dogs to better note their condition, while others share their bunks with the leader of the team."

The early Nome races influenced sled dog racing in several ways. Through trial and error, Nome Kennel Club officials established many of the racing rules used today. These rules include the individual start, which means teams leave the starting line one at a time, and strict rules against cruel treatment of dogs.

These early Nome races, with their rich prizes, also encouraged mushers to search for dogs that were especially good for racing. The first racing dogs were the same big, mixed breeds that worked the mines and carried the mail. Across the Bering Strait in Siberia, which is only two hundred miles west of Nome, Chukchi (pronounced CHOOK-chē) Eskimos bred dogs that were smaller than Alaskan dogs, but stronger and faster. A team of these blue-eyed dogs, which white people called Siberian huskies, were imported for the 1909 All Alaska Sweepstakes. The Siberian dogs didn't win that year, but by 1915 they were consistent winners.

One of the first men to race Siberian huskies was

Leonhard Seppala, who later participated in the serum run. This Norwegian, who had gone to Alaska during the gold rush, entered the 1914 All Alaska Sweepstakes and finished last. Despite this less than encouraging finish, he was inspired. For the next three years, he won the sweepstakes. Seppala and his team of Siberian huskies won many other Alaskan races, and he became a well-known champion.

The All Alaska Sweepstakes, like most sporting events across the country, was suspended when the United States entered World War I. A few years after the war ended, people again took up sled dog racing, and the sport's popularity spread. Many of the first races were long-distance runs that took a day or more to complete. After a few years, the faster and shorter sprint races, which usually takes less than an hour to complete, became popular, too.

In Fairbanks, the unofficial capital of Alaska's vast interior, organized sled dog racing began in 1927. That was the year of the Signal Corps Trophy Race, a tough, fifty-eight mile race round-trip from Fairbanks to the town of Summit. Other early Fairbanks races included the first competition for women, the seventeen-mile Ladies' Fromm Trophy Race. In 1936, Fairbanks hosted the first open North American Championship Sled Dog Race, which has become one of the sport's three most important races.

When sled dog racing began in Nome, Anchorage did not yet exist. But by the late 1930s, Anchorage had grown from a railroad construction site into a city.

Like log cabins and fur parkas, dog teams were a fixture of life on the northern frontier.

Each year, hundreds of fur buyers and trappers gathered for the annual Fur Rendezvous, several days of fur auctions, parties, and sled dog races. Today, the Fur Rendezvous, known locally as Rondy, is that city's biggest annual event. It features the World Championship Sled Dog Races, another one of the sport's top sprint races.

While no state in the lower forty-eight, which is an Alaskan term for the first forty-eight states, matched Alaska's enthusiasm for sled dog racing, the sport did spread. The first known organized race in the West was the American Dog Derby in 1917, in which five teams raced fifty-five miles from West Yellowstone, Montana, to Ashton, Idaho.

The derby became part of a western sprint-racing circuit that included Idaho, Montana, Wyoming, Utah, and California. Truckee, California, which is just north of Lake Tahoe, has been the locale of many movies about sled dogs. The most famous sled dog movie filmed there was *White Fang,* based on the Jack London novel of the same title.

Sled dog racing became popular in New England in the 1920s. The sport owes much of its early popularity in that region to Arthur Walden. As a young man, Walden, a New Hampshire native, traveled to the Klondike gold fields. He didn't find his fortune, but he spent several years in that remote section of northwestern Canada. He worked as a dog puncher, which is what the men were called who used sled dog teams to haul freight.

Just after World War I, Walden, with a team of sled dogs, returned to New Hampshire. He started a kennel named for his favorite lead dog, Chinook. He helped organize the New England Sled Dog Club, which became a model for sled dog clubs in other parts of the country.

Walden became the region's first racing champion. In 1922, he entered the first Eastern International Dog Sled Derby, a 123-mile race across the top of New Hampshire, from Berlin to Colebrook. He ran a team of nine half-breed Saint Bernards hitched single file and easily won the race in three days.

In 1926, Walden raced in and won the first Laconia World Championship Sled Dog Derby. That ninety-mile race in Laconia, New Hampshire, was one of the sport's most prestigious races for many years.

A famous race took place in 1927 between Walden, champion musher of New England, and Leonhard Seppala, champion musher of Alaska. Seppala, an Eskimo helper, and forty-four Siberian huskies had been touring the lower forty-eight. When the tour ended at New York City's Madison Square Garden, Walden invited Seppala up to his New Hampshire farm.

Because both men were professional sled dog racers who had never raced against each other, it was no surprise that Seppala and his host agreed to race. The event took place at the resort town of Poland Spring, Maine.

Few New Englanders gave Seppala a chance of winning. His Siberian huskies were runts compared with Walden's half-breed Saint Bernards. Also, Seppala's team had not been active, so his dogs weren't in good racing condition. The New Englanders didn't know that Seppala was similarly unimpressed by Walden's dogs, which he considered big, awkward mongrels.

Despite the Alaskan champion's confidence, it wasn't an easy race. At the start, his team ignored the trail and bolted for a nearby barn. It was embarrassing. This famous musher from Alaska, onlookers were saying, couldn't handle his dogs. His team got away from him a second time during the race. And he was delayed again when he stopped to help another racer catch a runaway

A mixed-breed team in an early All Alaska Sweepstakes before Siberian huskies became popular racing dogs.

team. Despite these problems, Seppala won seven minutes ahead of Walden. This impressive race helped Siberian huskies become popular racing dogs in the East.

Both Walden and Seppala contributed a great deal to sled dog racing in New England. For almost a decade, Walden promoted and popularized the sport in his native New Hampshire and in neighboring states. When he retired from sled dog racing, Walden sold his kennel and joined Admiral Richard Byrd's 1929 expedition to Antarctica. The expedition traveled by dog sled with

Walden as chief dog handler.

After winning the Poland Spring race, Seppala became part of New England sled dog racing lore. Seppala stayed in New England long enough to win the third Laconia World Championship in 1928. Before returning to the West, he and a partner started a kennel in Poland Spring where his famous lead dog, Togo, sired many other racing dogs.

Thanks to Seppala, Siberian huskies became the first champions of the trail. They were better than working dogs for racing. But the best racers were yet to come.

*A postcard from around the turn of the century features
Eskimo girls and sled dog puppies.*

3. A Dog of Many Breeds

Ever since Nome's early All Alaska Sweepstakes races, mushers have been trying to breed the perfect racing sled dog. Today, most racing sled dogs are mixed breeds with either Alaskan malamute or Siberian husky, or both, in their family trees. These two dogs are naturals for pulling sleds because for several thousand years they were bred for that purpose by Arctic Eskimos.

The Alaskan malamute stands twenty-four inches at the shoulders and weighs sixty to seventy pounds. Malamutes are usually a shade of gray or black with white markings. The breed is one of five dog breeds native to North America. They were bred by northern Alaskan Eskimos known as Malemutes, spelled with an "e" instead of a second "a." These people and their dogs were often mentioned in the journals of early explorers in Alaska.

The Siberian husky stands twenty-two inches at the shoulder and weighs forty to fifty pounds. Its color tends to be black, gray, white, or russet with a variety of markings. Many Siberian huskies have pale blue, almond-shaped eyes. The dogs were bred by Chukchi Eskimos in northeastern Siberia, a land similar to Alaska.

Both types of dogs were bred to pull sleds and to live comfortably in the Arctic. Both breeds have thick coats that keep them dry and warm during long, frigid winters. They shed much of their fur in the summer and regrow it for winter. Nature seems to tailor coats for each type of dog. Malamutes and Siberian huskies living in the lower forty-eight grow a thinner coat than their cousins in Alaska.

Because malamutes and Siberian huskies had lived for countless generations in isolated villages, both were

Eskimos relied on dogs for transportation until snowmobiles became popular in the 1960s.

very pure breeds. That changed during the gold rush years of the late nineteenth century when white people poured into Alaska and northwestern Canada, bringing with them thousands of dogs to work the gold mines.

Many of these dogs weren't strong enough to haul dirt and rock all day or to survive the harsh, cold winters. Hoping to produce stronger dogs, the miners bred their dogs with Indian and Eskimo dogs, which had long been accustomed to hard work and cold weather.

The first racing dogs were working dogs. These dogs pulled sleds in the winter and carried packs in the summer. They worked the mines and delivered the mail year-round. And when somebody decided to have a race, they ran the race.

At first, mushers were content with picking racing dogs from their own or their friends' working teams. These dogs were usually big and strong, but not necessarily fast. Working dogs didn't have to be fast. But as sled dog racing became more organized and more competitive, mushers began devoting more time and effort to breeding and training fast dogs just for racing. Since then, many different breeds have been combined to produce racing dogs.

Breeders often disagree on exactly what a good racing dog is, but they generally agree on some desirable characteristics. Racing dogs should have good feet, with pads tough enough to run long distances on ice and hard snow. Their bodies should be trim and well proportioned, and the dogs should be of uniform size. Dogs of a similar size and stride perform better as a team.

Mental attitude is more important, some breeders say, than physical qualities. Enthusiasm and a willingness to work in a team and to follow orders are all essential for sled dogs.

Breeding methods include line breeding and outbreeding. Line breeding involves mating dogs from the same extended family. For example, a seven-year-old champion racer might be bred with a two-year-old female dog, or bitch, that in human terms would be his granddaughter. By breeding related dogs, mushers hope to reproduce their dogs' good qualities. But they also knowingly risk reproducing some of the parents' inheritable problems, such as easily bruised footpads. Outbreeding is simply breeding two outstanding but unrelated dogs and hoping for the best.

Over the years, certain regions in Alaska, Canada, and the lower forty-eight have produced distinctive breeds of sled dogs. From Canada's Northwest Territories came Saint Bernard–sized dogs called Mackenzie River huskies, which were the sled dogs preferred by the Royal Canadian Mounted Police. The Mounties, as they were popularly called, were famous law enforcement officers on Canada's northwestern frontier. In eastern Canada, sled dogs and hounds were crossed to produce a breed of long-legged, short-haired racing dogs known as Quebec or Canadian hounds. Sled dog racers in Idaho crossed greyhounds and Irish setters to produce the Targee hound.

With so much crossbreeding, purebred Siberian huskies and malamutes almost disappeared. But Eva

Eva Seeley (at center), the famous dog breeder, awarding ribbons to two registered Siberian huskies.

Seeley rescued both breeds from extinction. After buying Arthur Walden's Chinook Kennel in the late 1920s, Seeley began breeding malamutes and Siberian huskies pure enough to be admitted, in 1930 and 1935, respectively, to the American Kennel Club. AKC registration helped both breeds become popular pets and show dogs. Some people use malamutes and Siberian huskies to pull a sled, but the dogs aren't popular for racing.

*Purebred malamutes are too big for competitive racing,
but they are popular pets and show dogs.*

Today, the most popular racing sled dog is the Alaskan husky, a crossbreed that often includes malamute and Siberian. Also popular for racing, particularly in the far north, is a type of sled dog that has several names. It's called either an Indian, village, or Eskimo dog. As the names imply, this dog is bred by Native Americans.

Some sled dog racers breed and train their own teams. These men and women are usually professionals who spend years developing a line of top-performing sled dogs.

Alaskan huskies, because of their mixed ancestry, are a variety of sizes and colors. This is a particularly handsome racing Alaskan husky.

A truck fitted with a dog carrier is basic equipment for Harris Dunlap (left) and other professional racers.

4. Training Racing Sled Dogs

Harris Dunlap is one of the best drivers, breeders, and trainers in sled dog racing. Harris has been racing dogs for over twenty-five years and has won hundreds of sprint races, including the sport's three biggest — the ALPO International Sled Dog Races in Saranac Lake, New York, the World Championship in Anchorage, and the Open North American Championship in Fairbanks.

Harris, his wife Ginger, and two of their five children live in Bakers Mills, New York, high in the Adirondack Mountains. Literally surrounded by their work, the Dunlaps' home sits inside a five-acre compound full of dog lots, dog houses, and, depending on the season, some one hundred to one hundred fifty sled dogs.

The Dunlaps travel the sprint racing circuit from New England to Alaska for three months a year, January through March. The rest of the year, they're at home breeding and training dogs to race and sell. Dunlap dogs, which sell for five hundred to fifteen hundred dollars each, are bought by racers all across the United

States, Canada, and Europe. No two racers train their dogs exactly the same, but, judging from the number of races won and the big demand for their dogs, the Dunlap method is quite successful.

Each year in April, immediately after the racing season, the Dunlaps begin nine months of conditioning, training, evaluating, and breeding their dogs. Also, the Dunlaps usually have thirty to fifty yearlings, which are dogs between one and two years old, and pups, which are dogs less than a year old, that need to be trained and evaluated for racing potential.

Curious and active, this pup shows promise as a future racing sled dog.

With his dogs' racing performances fresh in mind, April is a good month for Harris to evaluate his team's strengths and weaknesses. Like a coach, he studies his lineup to see if it can be improved by replacing dogs or switching positions.

It's also a good month to think about breeding. The Dunlaps want racing dogs that are tough, fast, persistent, and enthusiastic. Matching parents with these qualities, they hope to produce pups with the same strengths. A bitch bred in April will have pups by July.

When pups are born, usually in the spring or summer, they're immediately enrolled in what could be called the Dunlap school of sled dog training. First, to learn not to be afraid of people, the pups and their mother live next to the compound's front gate. There they see the Dunlaps, delivery people, and visitors coming and going. After the puppies are a few weeks old, they have the run of the compound. They are very friendly and will follow anyone around, playfully nipping at a shoelace or a pants cuff.

After the puppies are several months old, they begin preparing for the hard work and discipline of racing. Among their first training exercises are long walks. The Dunlaps take eight to ten dogs hiking over several miles of fields and forests, hills and rocks. The young dogs roam freely. A couple of older dogs go along to help keep order. These "grown-ups" obey orders promptly, and the younger dogs follow. Hikes, Harris says, generally toughen up the dogs. Harris doesn't expect his pups to start pulling in a team until they are nearly a year old.

When there is no snow, Harris uses a rig to train and condition his dogs.

In May, the Dunlaps begin gig training, which teaches the yearlings how to pull and how to work in a team. The gig, which is also called a rig, is a three-wheel cart used for pulling exercises when there is no snow. This custom-built cart, unlike a sled, has a steering device and a hydraulic brake. Harris likes to use a fairly heavy gig so that, right away, the dogs learn to pull hard.

For gig training, the Dunlaps use an apprenticeship method that allows beginners to learn the ropes by working with experienced dogs. In a team of seven or

eight dogs, yearlings are paired with veterans. The experienced team members, Harris explains, help teach the pups. When the older dogs respond to the commands, they force the younger dogs to respond the same way.

Harris looks for young dogs that run hard, have good strides, and good attitudes. Speed is not important until the yearlings have done a lot of pulling.

In these first training sessions, mileage is less important than the number of times the young dogs pull a sled. It's surprising, Harris says, how much they can learn in ten hookups. The trainer, he cautions, shouldn't exceed what the dogs can take, either physically or mentally. The puppies have had no education, so it's important to be patient and forgiving. Also, the training should be fun to allow the dogs to develop a good attitude about both training and racing.

By June, after just a few weeks of training, the young dogs begin to understand commands. They are developing endurance and can run in harness for about two miles. Harris rotates the dogs to all positions in the team.

The dogs are taught to run at different speeds on an exercise wheel that controls their pace. Hitched to this wheel, they trot around and around in a circle for up to three hours. Like horses or human racers, the dogs must race at a measured pace so they don't tire too quickly. On the exercise wheel, they learn the meaning of "Easy" and "Are you ready?" — Harris's commands to slow down and speed up.

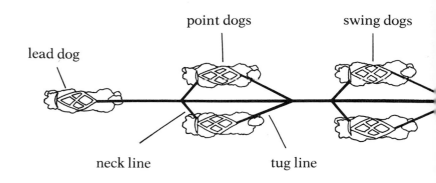

The four positions in a sled dog team are lead, point, swing, and wheel. There can be one or two lead dogs. In Alaska some terms are different. The dogs directly behind the lead are called

Training sessions are important for teaching yearlings to be racing dogs and for conditioning older, experienced dogs for the upcoming racing season.

Every couple of months, Harris likes to see how fast his team can run. In the summer, these speed runs are done in the cool, early mornings. A cool temperature is important because it keeps the dogs from overheating, which can be fatal.

In September, with the racing season just four months away, the training gets tougher. During the month, Harris and Ginger take their dogs through a minimum of fifteen workouts. These include ten- to fifteen-mile walks on the exercise wheel at about seven miles an hour and gig runs of two to four miles over rolling and flat terrain.

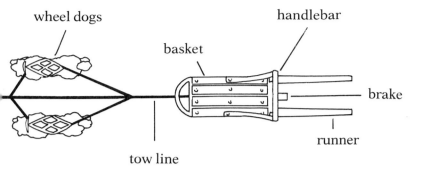

wheel dogs

handlebar

basket

brake

runner

tow line

swing dogs, and those between the swing and wheel positions are called team dogs. The dogs are connected to the sled by the tow line and guided only by voice commands from the driver.

In October, with cooler weather, there are more outings. Training sessions include three to six miles on the gig and fifteen to twenty miles on the exercise wheel. The Dunlaps train nearly every other day, which keeps the dogs strong; the forty-eight hours between workouts lessens the chance of injury.

In November, the Dunlaps train on the gig for four- to ten-mile runs. The dogs still walk fifteen to twenty miles on the exercise wheel. Training sessions, like many races, are now scheduled back-to-back. The dogs work two days, then rest one day. Toward the end of the month, the Adirondacks get the first snow of the season, the gig is put away, and the dogs are hitched to sleds.

This is a good time to pair the dogs, matching them by both stride and personality. Dogs have different per-

Harris Dunlap's exercise wheel was originally designed for horses. Harris applies horse breeding and training methods to the breeding and training of racing sled dogs.

sonalities and, like people, they don't always get along. When the Dunlaps find two dogs that work well together in harness, they pair them in other situations, too. The dogs live next to each other in the kennel and share the same cage on the truck. That helps them to become comfortable with each other and to work better together.

November is also when Harris grades his dogs. Like a football coach, he decides which dogs will be on the team, and he divides the team into squads. One squad will be best for eight-mile races, another squad for fifteen-mile races. These lineups can change at any time depending on performance. Some dogs will be hurt during the season, others will become better racers, and some will turn out to be poor racers.

In December, with the first race just a few weeks away, the training gets harder. The Dunlaps run their team about 175 miles in eighteen outings. With the strain of harder workouts, some of the dogs begin to perform poorly. Harris thinks of ways to perk up his team. A few days of rest followed by a short, easy run often makes the dogs feel better.

When the racing season starts in January, each race counts as a training run. For example, Harris might be in four races, each consisting of two heats of fifteen miles each. After each race, the team rests a couple of days and then trains a couple of days. Counting the races, there would be sixteen training sessions that month.

Sled dogs perform better at the beginning of the season than at the end of the season. Likewise, dogs do better on the first day of a race than on the second or third day. Harris watches his team carefully, paying close attention to his dogs' mental and physical condition, and he doesn't decide on a lineup until just before a race. Here are some of the signs Harris looks for:

· A dog in good condition barks, is alert, behaves well, responds to commands, is frisky, likes company, eats briskly, and is anxious to run.

· A dog that's not in good condition is remote, ignores orders or obeys reluctantly, seems irritable, avoids people, and eats and drinks little.

· A dog in distress makes no noise, avoids people and other dogs, is unresponsive, and doesn't eat or drink.

An important part of training and racing is diet. Like all good athletes, sled dogs need to eat properly. There is much debate among professional sled dog racers about what makes the best diet. The Dunlaps have experimented with diets for more than a decade, and now they feed their dogs a mixture of chicken and pork.

The dogs are fed different amounts of food during the year. Racing dogs should be lean but not skinny. In the nonracing season, they are fed one can of food a day. When conditioning begins in the fall, the amount of food is doubled or tripled depending on the weather, the type of training, and the amount of stress.

As the Dunlaps prove, sled dog training and racing have become much more demanding and sophisticated since the early Nome races. A lot of work, time, and expense go into producing top sled dogs. Despite these demands, sled dog racing is not a sport for dedicated professionals only. Indeed, most of the people who enjoy the sport are amateurs.

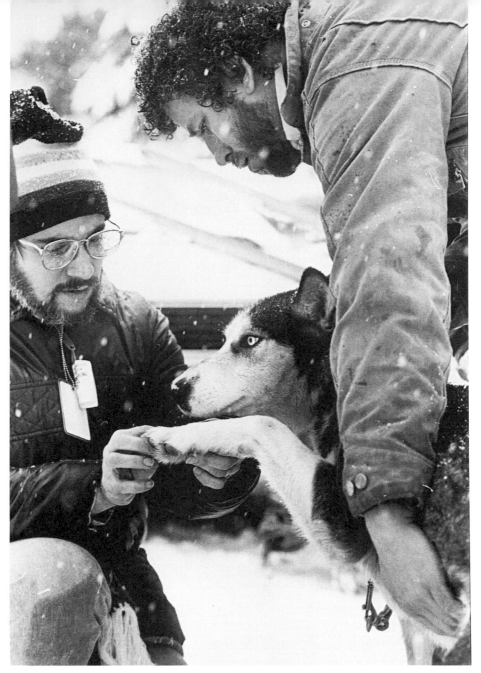

A veterinarian checks a husky's paw. Sled dogs are well cared for.

5. Sled Dog Racing Today

Professionals and amateurs, men and women, adults and children can all enjoy sled dog racing. Sled dog races are held from coast to coast in Canada and the snowy states of the United States.

Basically, there are two kinds of sled dog races, long-distance and sprint. Long-distance races, which are usually thirty miles or longer, are popular in Alaska. The best-known long-distance race is the Iditarod. Another tough but less-known race is the Yukon Quest. This is a thousand-mile race held in March between Fairbanks, Alaska, and Fort Dawson, Yukon Territory.

Long-distance racing is expensive, exhausting, and dangerous. For example, the Iditarod Trail International Sled Dog Race costs over one million dollars annually. For months, hundreds of people — veterinarians, pilots, checkpoint officials — plan and manage the race.

Long-distance racing is demanding of drivers, too. A team running the Iditarod spends ten thousand dollars or more on supplies, entry fees, and transportation. Mushers also face a variety of dangers such as wild animals, frostbite, and hypothermia. They go for days with little sleep or food. But it's these challenges that make long-distance racing exciting.

Sprint racing is by far the most popular form of sled dog racing for professionals and amateurs alike. Sprint races are usually no longer than thirty miles and sometimes as short as three miles. The races, or meets, as they are often called, are divided into classes defined by the number of dogs in a team and the length of the course. A race is usually run in two or three heats. For example, a twenty-mile course would be run once a day for three days. The times for each heat are combined, and the team with the fastest total time wins the event.

Today, three races are generally considered sprint racing's top events. They offer the sport's biggest money prizes and attract the best racers. Borrowing a term from horse racing, these three are referred to as the "triple crown" of sled dog racing.

The first of the big races is the ALPO International Sled Dog Races at Saranac Lake, New York. This race, held in late January every year, features prize money of some fifty thousand dollars and attracts over one hundred drivers.

The second race of the "triple crown" is the World Championship Sled Dog Race in Anchorage. This race, held annually in late February, also attracts more than one hundred of the sport's best racers, who compete for over fifty thousand dollars in prize money.

Dogs, harness, and sleds are all carried to meets in specially designed trucks.

The third big race, which is held at the end of March, is the Open North American Championship in Fairbanks. Although the prize money is only about half as much as for the other two top races, the North American is an important race that attracts many of the same competitors.

*Jean Bryer, one of the sport's best women racers, at the
Laconia (NH) World Sled Dog Derby.*

Nowhere is sled dog racing more popular than in Alaska, where it's the official state sport. Towns and villages all across that vast state, which is twice the size of Texas, hold races with cash prizes. There is professional racing most winter weekends at tracks in both Anchorage and Fairbanks.

Outside of Alaska, professional races are held in various parts of the northern United States. The ALPO International Sled Dog Races at Saranac Lake, New York, is the lower forty-eight's biggest annual race. For many years, Laconia, New Hampshire, was considered the sled dog racing capital of the East. Its annual World Championship in February is the Northeast's oldest race.

The second most active racing state is Minnesota. Top racers from across North America compete in the state's biggest race, the mid-January All American Championship Race in the city of Ely (pronounced EE-ly).

For every professional sled dog racer, there are a dozen amateurs. For every professional race, there are dozens of amateur meets. These meets are sponsored by local sled dog racing clubs coast-to-coast in all of the Canadian provinces, in every northern state, and in some states as far south as Maryland and Arizona.

Although there are a lot of clubs, only a few thousand people are sled dog drivers. For these people, both professionals and amateurs, dogs are a very big part of their lives. Whether they own three or three dozen sled dogs, they spend a lot of time feeding, training, nursing, and talking about their team.

A sled dog team is a family affair. Mother, father, and children help care for the dogs. They watch them grow from cute puppies to energetic adolescents to — if raised right — serious, hardworking adults.

Weekend sled dog meets are places for people to get together, talk, and share their enthusiasm for the animals and the sport. To enter one of these meets doesn't require much racing experience or a large team of dogs. There is competition for everyone, veterans and beginners alike. Men and women compete equally. Racers under eighteen often compete in age categories.

Like the professional meets, amateur races are di-

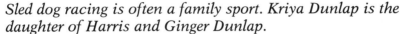

Sled dog racing is often a family sport. Kriya Dunlap is the daughter of Harris and Ginger Dunlap.

George Attla, an Athabascan Indian from Alaska, is one of sled dog racing's most famous drivers.

vided into classes determined by the length of the race and the number of dogs in a team. There are usually four classes of competition: unlimited, eight-dog, six-dog, and three-dog.

The biggest teams are in the unlimited class, where a driver can run twelve to sixteen dogs. Drivers usually run the maximum number of dogs allowed. Trail distances vary from twelve to thirty miles. Many of the best known racers, such as Harris Dunlap, George Attla, Cindy Molberg Bicknell, and Dr. Roland Lombard, race in the unlimited class.

The six-dog class is often the most popular event for

drivers. In this class, there are three to six dogs in a team, which is enough dog power for a thrilling ride.

Meets are held on winter weekends, usually at a park or farm with plenty of open space for trails. Families arrive in trucks topped with their dog carriers, harnesses, and sleds. The meet is a friendly affair with lots of visiting and talking while the racers prepare their sleds and dogs.

A half hour before each race, the dogs are put into harness. A few minutes before his or her turn, the driver leads the team to the starting chute. In the chute, handlers hold the excited team while the driver gives the dogs pats and words of encouragement — a pep talk.

Some sled dogs get very excited about racing.

Seconds before the start, the driver hops on the sled's runners. The announcer counts down, five, four, three, two, one, and then commands, "Go, driver." The dogs, heads down and legs outstretched, dash down the trail.

All concentration, the driver watches closely to make sure the dogs are running well. He or she is constantly looking for tangled harness or signs of bruised paws. As the driver, balanced on the sled's runners, shouts commands, the team turns right or left, slows down or speeds up. After months of training, driver and dogs work together like a precision drill team.

Win or lose, most people race sled dogs for fun. Racing is too demanding and too costly, and the cash prizes are too few and too small, for people to race for any other reason. Sled dog racing is not for everyone, but it's a truly unique and exciting sport for people who like the winter outdoors and who love dogs.

Mushers and their dogs develop strong bonds.

For More Information

Organizations

The organizations listed below should be able to provide information about sled dog related activities in their regions. Some of these organizations publish newsletters with information about races and other club activities.

The International Sled Dog Racing Association, which is the largest organization for sled dog enthusiasts, publishes two newsletters, *INFO* and, for young members, *Howl*.

Alaska Sled Dog Racing Association
P.O. Box 110569
Anchorage, AK 99511

Alberta Sled Dog Association
Site 1, P.O. Box 20
Rural Route 2
Tolfield, Alberta, Canada T0B4J0

Great Lakes Sled Dog Association
1846 Hamilton Highway
Adrian, MI 49221

Iditarod Trail Committee
Pouch X
Wasilla, AK 99687

International Sled Dog Racing Association
P.O. Box 446
Nordman, Idaho 83848

Lakes Region Sled Dog Club
P.O. Box 382
Laconia, NH 03247

Mason-Dixon Sled Dog Racing Association
9215 Baltimore National Pike
Middletown, MD 21769

New England Sled Dog Club
RFD 4, Box 305B
Manchester, NH 03100

Sierra Nevada Dog Drivers
1763 Indian Valley Road
Novato, CA 94947

Publications

Sports periodicals often cover the big sled dog races. Racing news and general information of interest to racing enthusiasts are provided by two monthly newsletters.

Alaskan Gangline
P.O. Box 870650
Wasilla, AK 99687

Team & Trail
P.O. Box 128
Center Harbor, NH 03226-0128

Photo Credits

The photographs in this book are from the following sources:

ALPO/Wide World: endpapers, pages 2, 22, 41, 54, 57, 58, 60, 61, 62, 64.

Photos © by Greg Anderson/Detroit News: pages 11, 18–19.

Photo © by Isabelle Bich/Gamma Liaison: page 15.

Photos © by Walter Chandoha: pages 46, 50.

Photos © by Michael Cooper: pages 42, 44.

Photo © by Jeff Schultz/Gamma Liaison: page 21.

Photos © by Evelyn M. Shafer: pages 39, 40.

University of Washington: Photos by Hegg, page 26 (negative number 2467) and page 29 (negative number 578). Photo by Lomen Brothers, pages 32–33 (negative number VW#8180). Photos by F. Nowell, page 34 (negative number VW#8182) and page 36 (negative number VW#8181).

Index

Page numbers in *italics* refer to illustrations.